FLUTE

101 CLASSICAL THEMES

Available for
FLUTE, CLARINET, ALTO SAX, TENOR SAX, TRUMPET,
HORN, TROMBONE, VIOLIN, VIOLA, CELLO

ISBN 978-1-4950-5623-9

HAL•LEONARD®
CORPORATION
7777 W. Bluemound Rd. P.O. Box 13819 Milwaukee, WI 53213

In Australia Contact:
Hal Leonard Australia Pty. Ltd.
4 Lentara Court
Cheltenham, Victoria, 3192 Australia
Email: ausadmin@halleonard.com.au

CONTENTS

1812 OVERTURE
(Theme)

FLUTE

PYOTR IL'YICH TCHAIKOVSKY

Allegro vivace

AIR
from WATER MUSIC

GEORGE FRIDERIC HANDEL

Andante

AIR ON THE G STRING

from ORCHESTRAL SUITE NO. 3

JOHANN SEBASTIAN BACH

ARIOSO

from CANTATA 156

FLUTE

JOHANN SEBASTIAN BACH

AVE MARIA

based on "Prelude in C Major" by Johann Sebastian Bach

FLUTE

CHARLES GOUNOD

ANDANTE CANTABILE

from STRING QUARTET NO. 1

FLUTE

PYOTR IL'YICH TCHAIKOVSKY

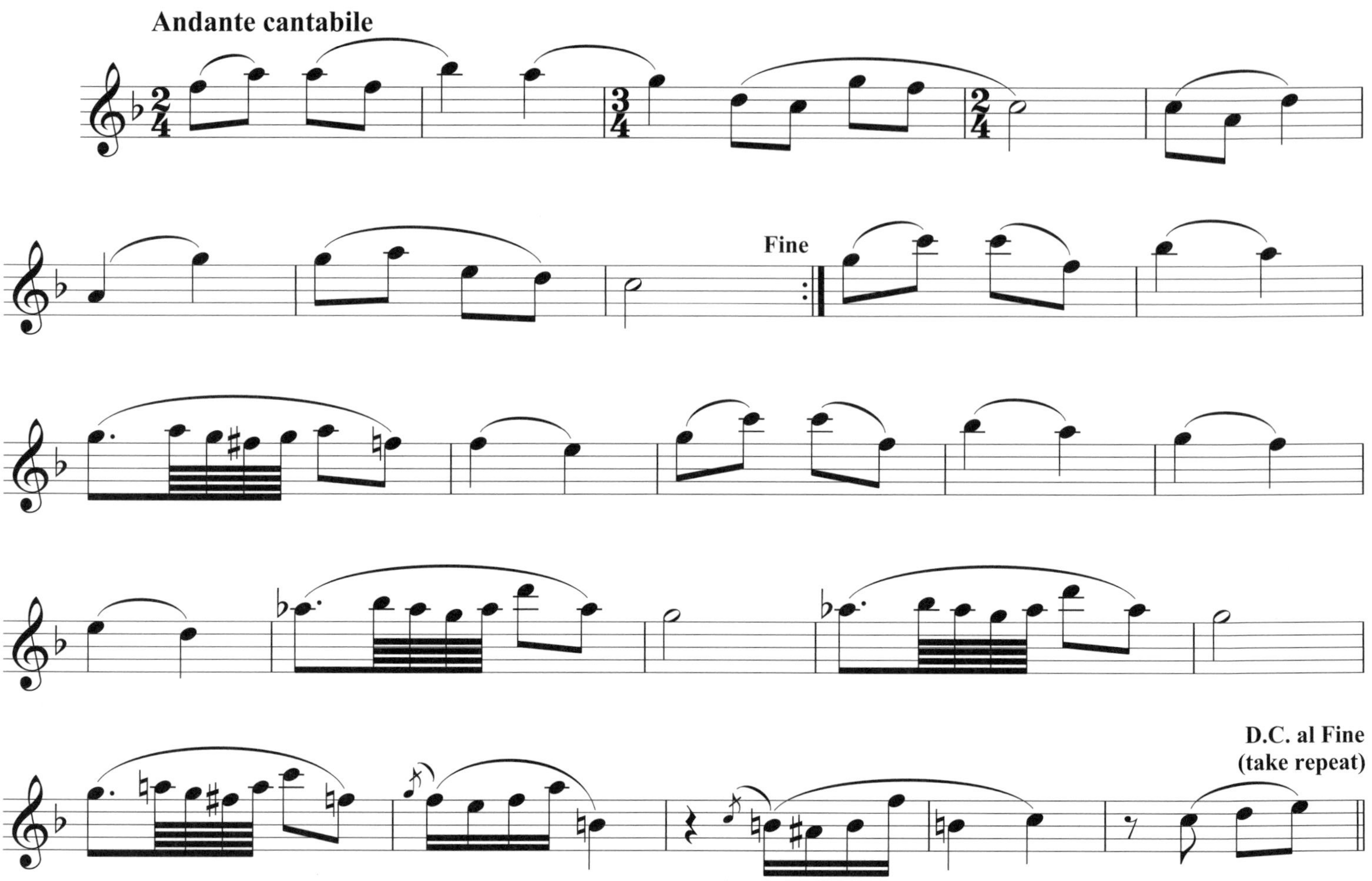

AVE MARIA

FRANZ SCHUBERT

BIST DU BEI MIR

Copyright © 2016 HAL LEONARD CORPORATION
International Copyright Secured All Rights Reserved

GOTTFRIED HEINRICH STÖZEL
(previously attributed to J.S. Bach)

AVE VERUM CORPUS

FLUTE

Copyright © 2016 HAL LEONARD CORPORATION
International Copyright Secured All Rights Reserved

WOLFGANG AMADEUS MOZART

BADINERIE

from ORCHESTRAL SUITE NO. 2

FLUTE

Copyright © 2016 HAL LEONARD CORPORATION
International Copyright Secured All Rights Reserved

JOHANN SEBASTIAN BACH

Quickly, lightly
tr

BARCAROLLE
from THE TALES OF HOFFMANN

FLUTE

JACQUES OFFENBACH

BLUE DANUBE WALTZ

FLUTE

JOHANN STRAUSS, JR.

BOURRÉE IN E MINOR
from LUTE SUITE IN E MINOR

FLUTE

JOHANN SEBASTIAN BACH

BRANDENBURG CONCERTO NO. 3
(First Movement Theme)

JOHANN SEBASTIAN BACH

BRANDENBURG CONCERTO NO. 5

(First Movement Theme)

JOHANN SEBASTIAN BACH

Moderately

BRIDAL CHORUS

from LOHENGRIN

FLUTE

RICHARD WAGNER

CLAIR DE LUNE
from SUITE BERGAMASQUE

FLUTE

CLAUDE DEBUSSY

CAN CAN

from ORPHEUS IN THE UNDERWORLD

FLUTE

JACQUES OFFENBACH

Allegretto moderato

CANON IN D

JOHANN PACHELBEL

Adagio

CARO MIO BEN

TOMMASO GIORDANI

Larghetto

DANCE OF THE HOURS

from LA GIOCONDA

FLUTE

AMILCARE PONCHIELLI

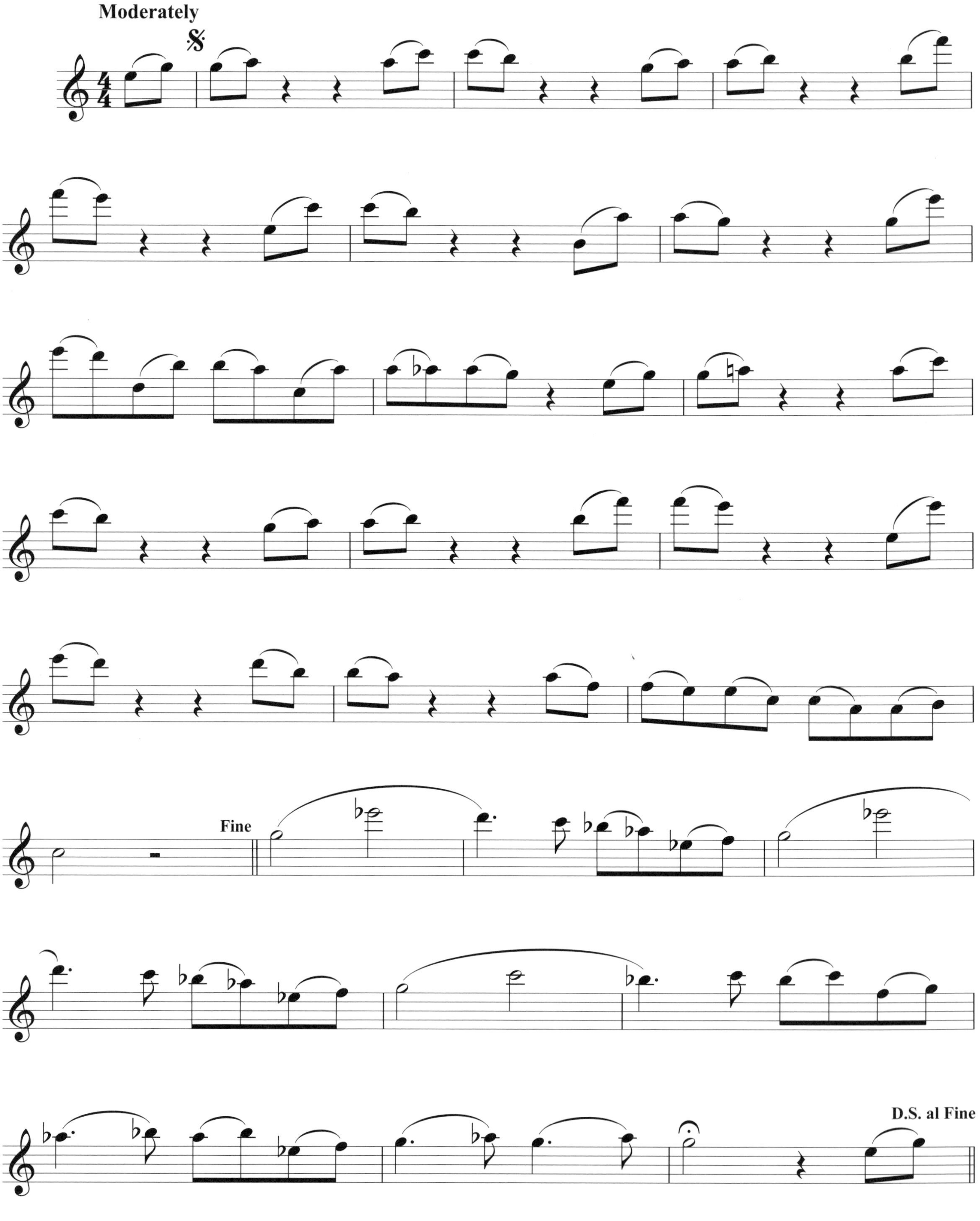
Moderately
Fine
D.S. al Fine

DANCE OF THE REED-FLUTES

from THE NUTCRACKER

FLUTE

PYOTR IL'YICH TCHAIKOVSKY

DANCE OF THE SPIRITS

from ORFEO ED EURIDICE

FLUTE

CHRISTOPH WILLIBALD VON GLUCK

DANCE OF THE SUGAR PLUM FAIRY

from THE NUTCRACKER

PYOTR IL'YICH TCHAIKOVSKY

EINE KLEINE NACHTMUSIK

(First Movement Theme)

WOLFGANG AMADEUS MOZART

EVENING PRAYER

from HANSEL AND GRETEL

FLUTE

ENGELBERT HUMPERDINCK

THE FLIGHT OF THE BUMBLEBEE

NICOLAI RIMSKY-KORSAKOV

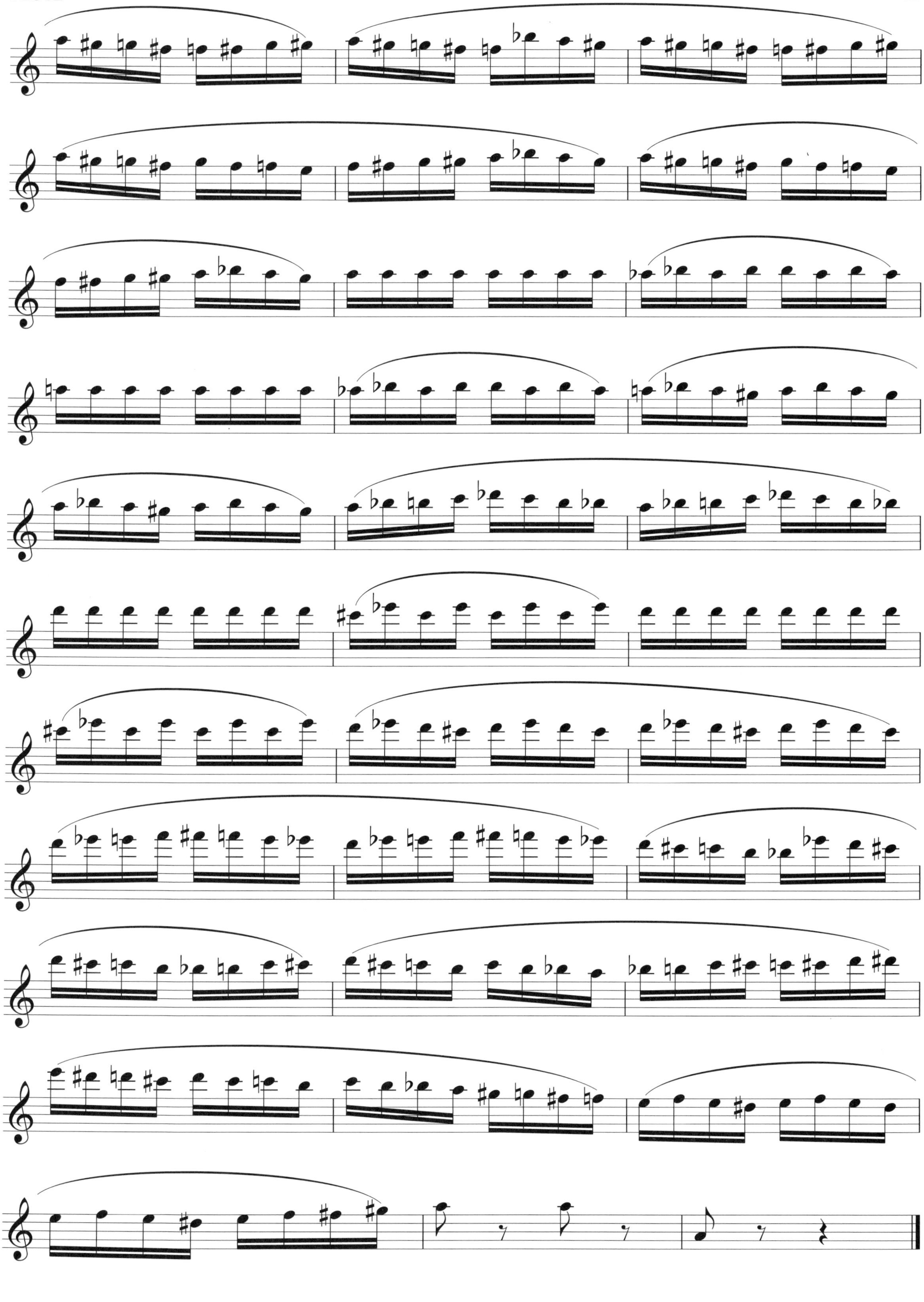

EINE KLEINE NACHTMUSIK

(Second Movement Theme: "Romanze")

FLUTE

WOLFGANG AMADEUS MOZART

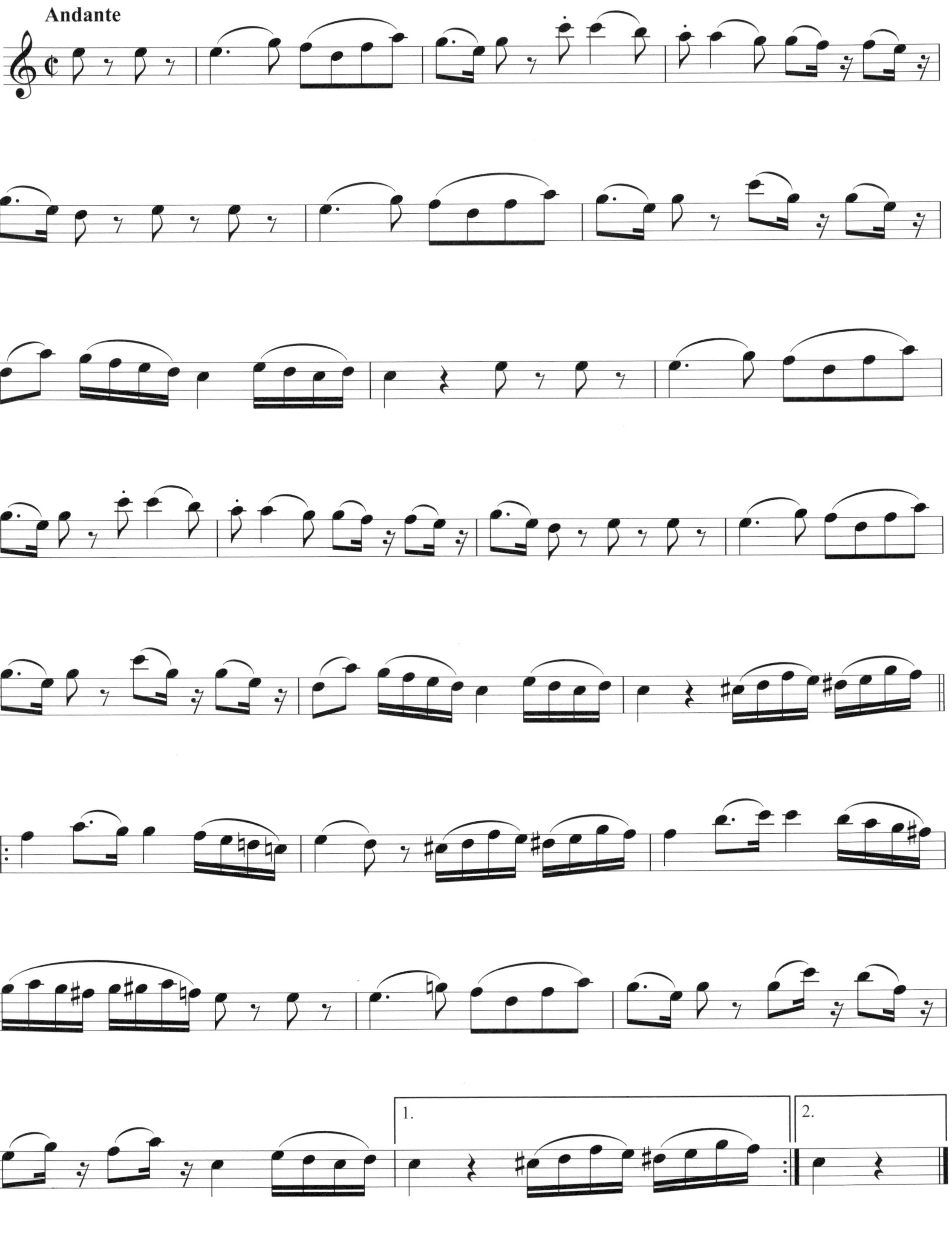

FLOWER DUET
from LAKMÉ

FLUTE

LÉO DELIBES

Andantino con moto

FUNERAL MARCH

(Marche funèbre)

from PIANO SONATA NO. 2

FLUTE

FRÉDÉRIC CHOPIN

FUNERAL MARCH OF A MARIONETTE

FLUTE

CHARLES GOUNOD

FÜR ELISE
(Bagatelle No. 25)

FLUTE

LUDWIG VAN BEETHOVEN

THE GREAT GATE OF KIEV
from PICTURES AT AN EXHIBITION

MODEST MUSSORGSKY

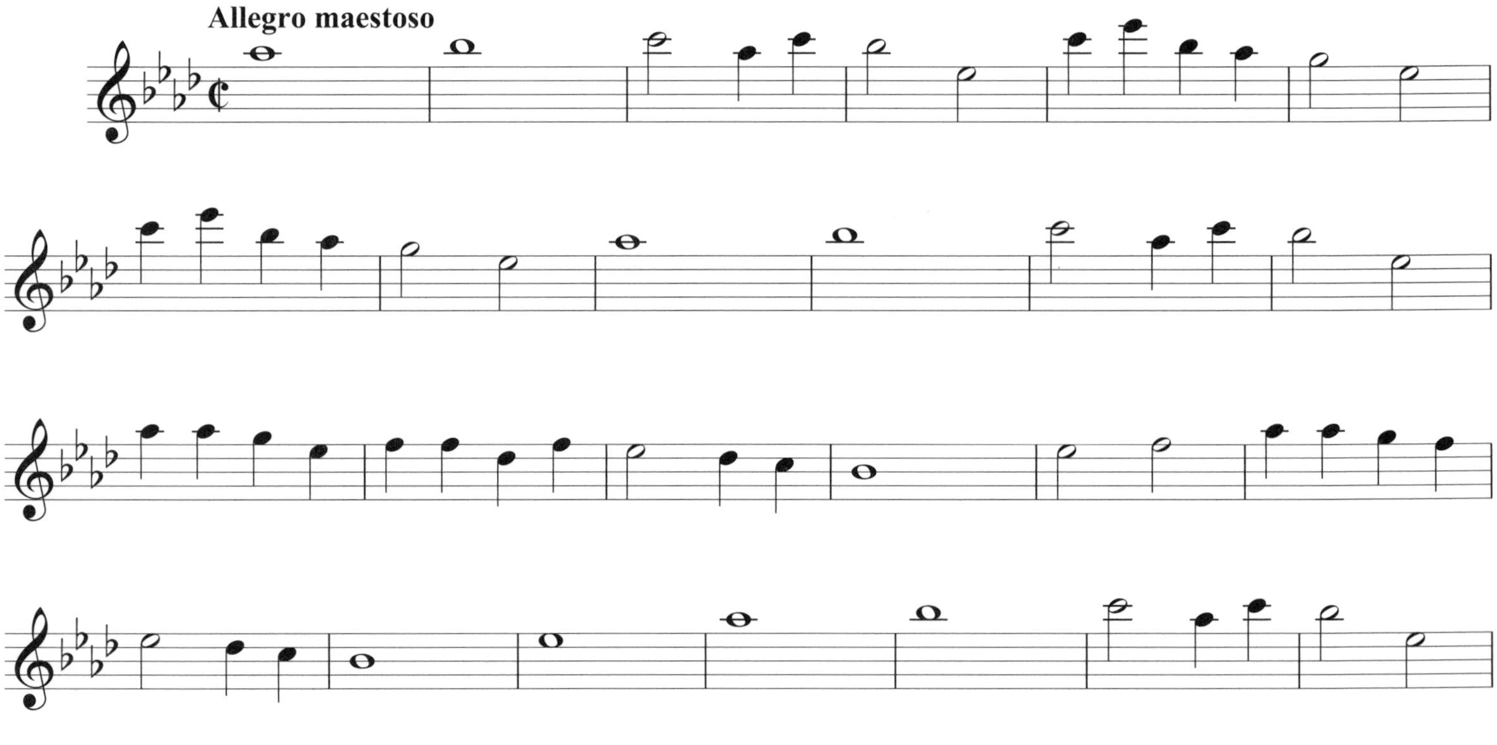

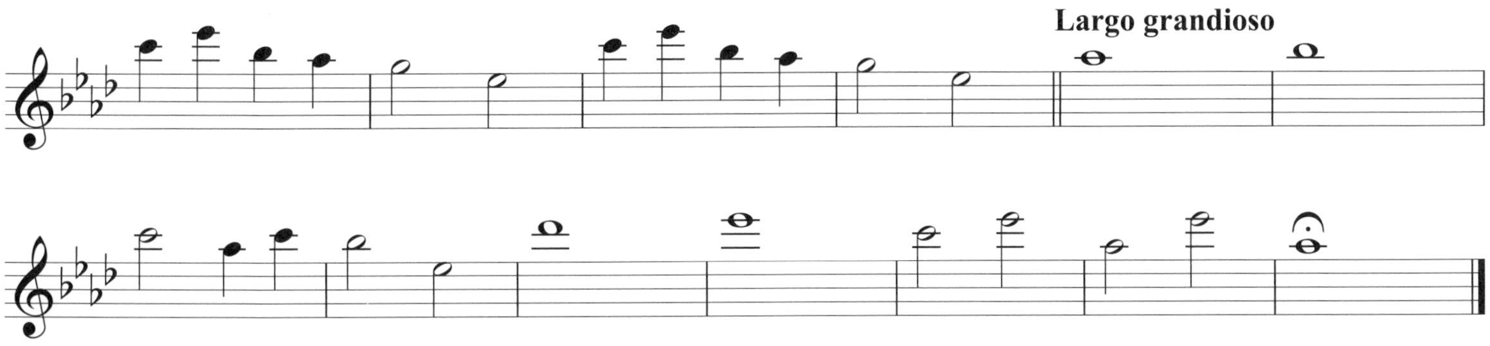
Largo grandioso

GYMNOPÉDIE NO. 1

ERIC SATIE

Lent et douloureux
1.
2.

HABANERA

from CARMEN

FLUTE

GEORGES BIZET

Allegro quasi andantino

THE HAPPY FARMER

from ALBUM FOR THE YOUNG

FLUTE

ROBERT SCHUMANN

Brightly, cheerfully

THE HARMONIOUS BLACKSMITH

from HARPSICHORD SUITE NO. 5

GEORGE FRIDERIC HANDEL

Andante

HORNPIPE
from WATER MUSIC

FLUTE

GEORGE FRIDERIC HANDEL

Allegro maestoso

HUNGARIAN DANCE NO. 5

FLUTE

JOHANNES BRAHMS

HALLELUJAH CHORUS

from MESSIAH

FLUTE

GEORGE FRIDERIC HANDEL

Allegro

INTERMEZZO

from CAVALLERIA RUSTICANA

PIETRO MASCAGNI

Andante

JERUSALEM

HUBERT PARRY

Moderately

IN THE HALL OF THE MOUNTAIN KING

from PEER GYNT

FLUTE

EDVARD GRIEG

JESU, JOY OF MAN'S DESIRING

from CANTATA 147

FLUTE

JOHANN SEBASTIAN BACH

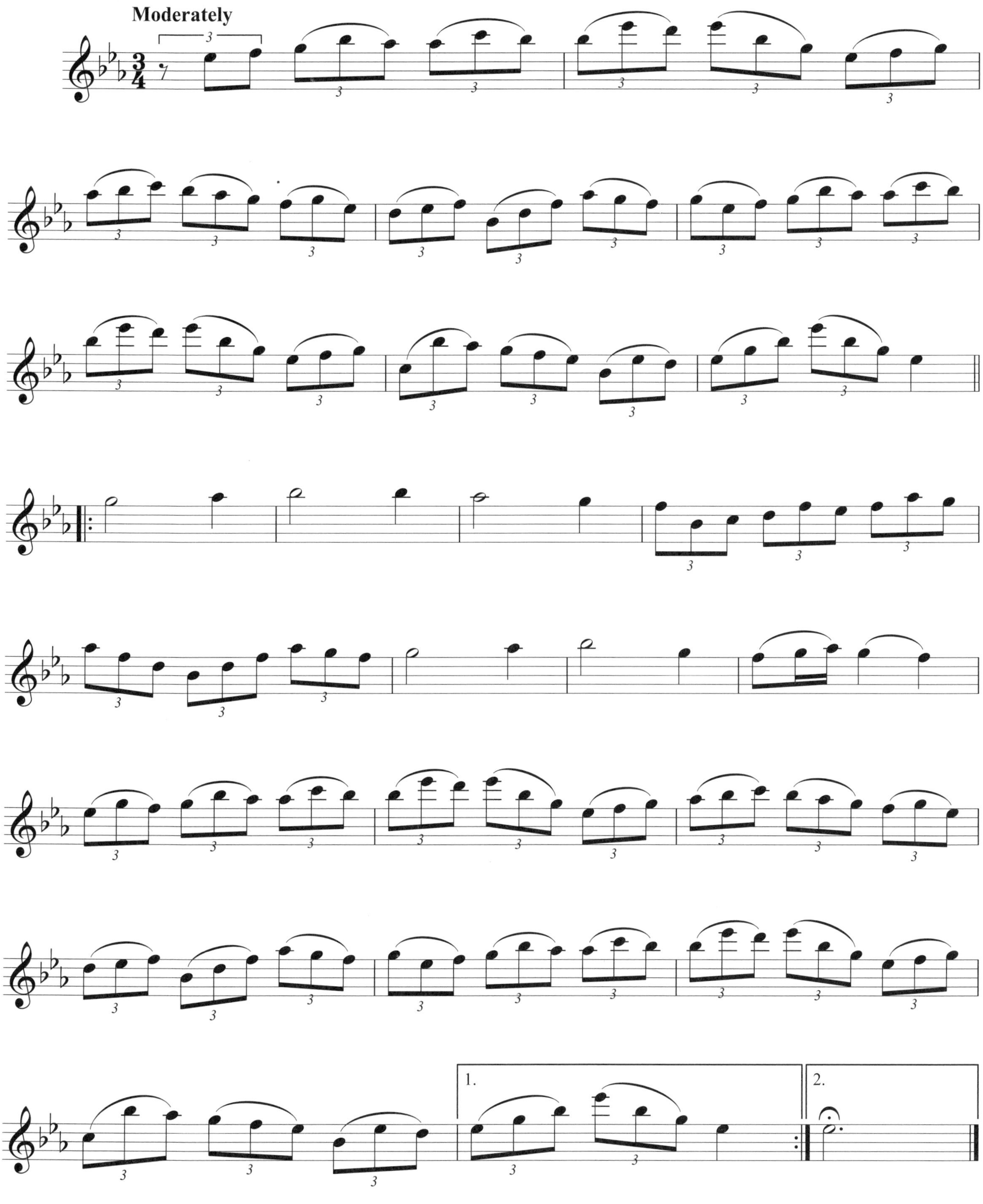

LARGO

from XERXES

FLUTE

GEORGE FRIDERIC HANDEL

LAUDATE DOMINUM

from VESPERAE SOLENNES DE CONFESSORE

FLUTE

WOLFGANG AMADEUS MOZART

LULLABY
(Wiegenlied)

FLUTE

JOHANNES BRAHMS

Moderately, tenderly

LIEBESTRAUM

FRANZ LISZT

Poco allegro

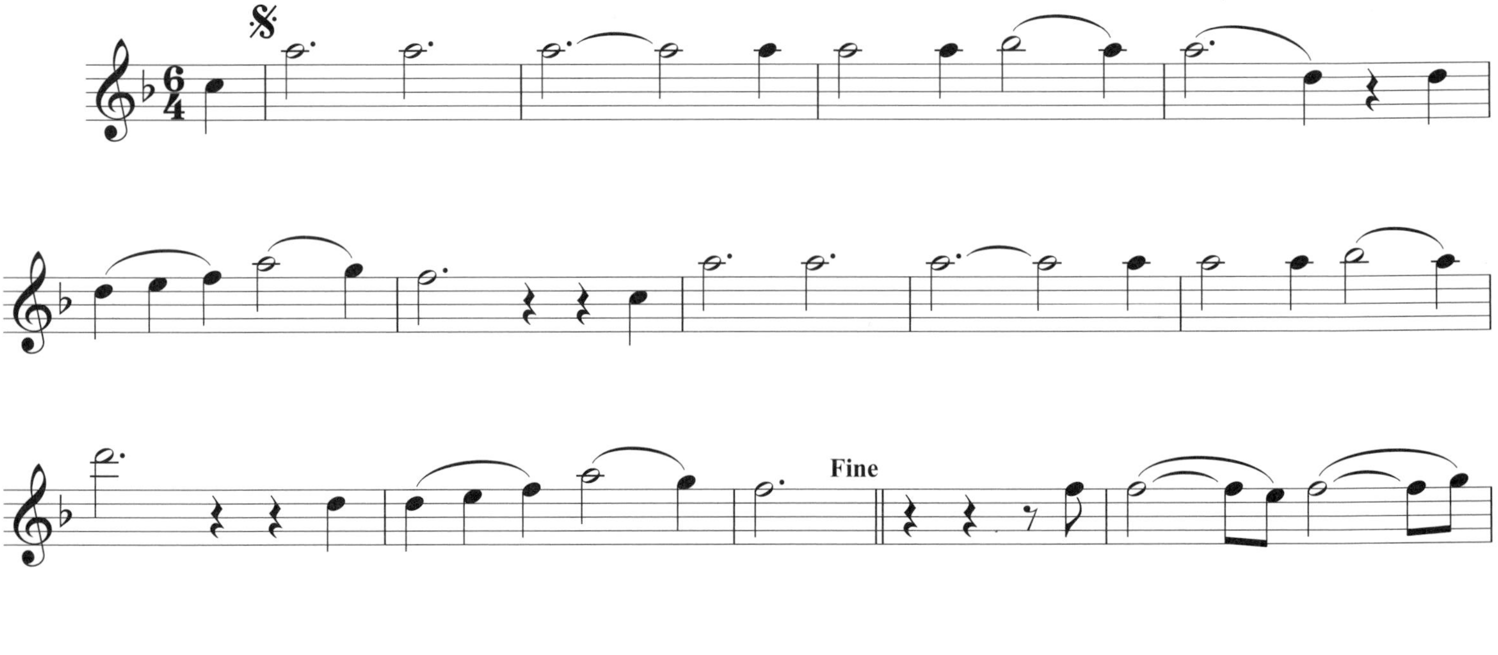

MELODY IN F

ANTON RUBINSTEIN

MARCH

from THE NUTCRACKER

FLUTE

PYOTR IL'YICH TCHAIKOVSKY

MARCHE SLAVE

FLUTE

PYOTR IL'YICH TCHAIKOVSKY

MINUET

from STRING QUINTET NO. 5

FLUTE

LUIGI BOCCHERINI

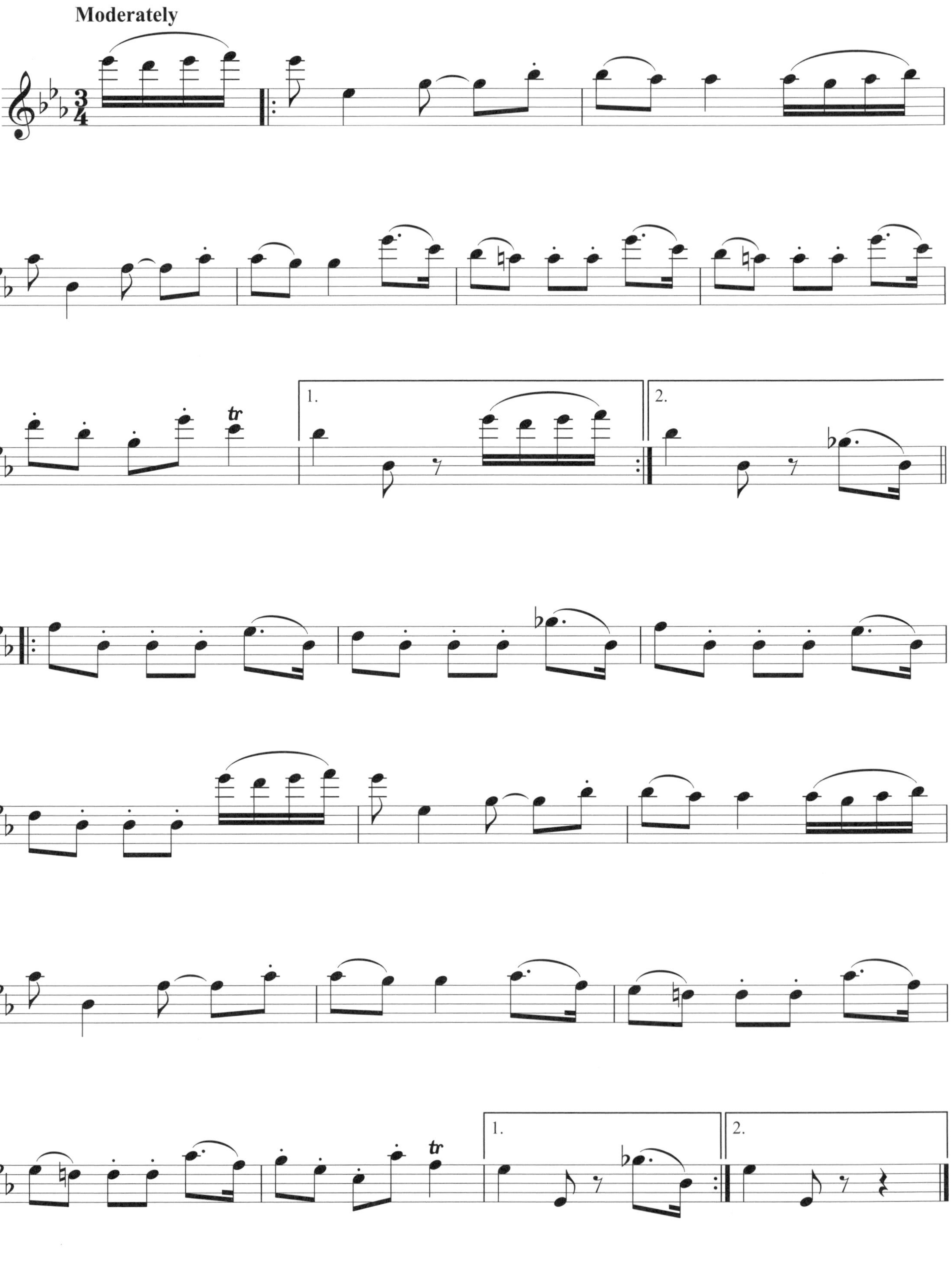

OVERTURE

from THE NUTCRACKER

FLUTE

PYOTR IL'YICH TCHAIKOVSKY

MORNING

from PEER GYNT

FLUTE

EDVARD GRIEG

Allegretto pastorale

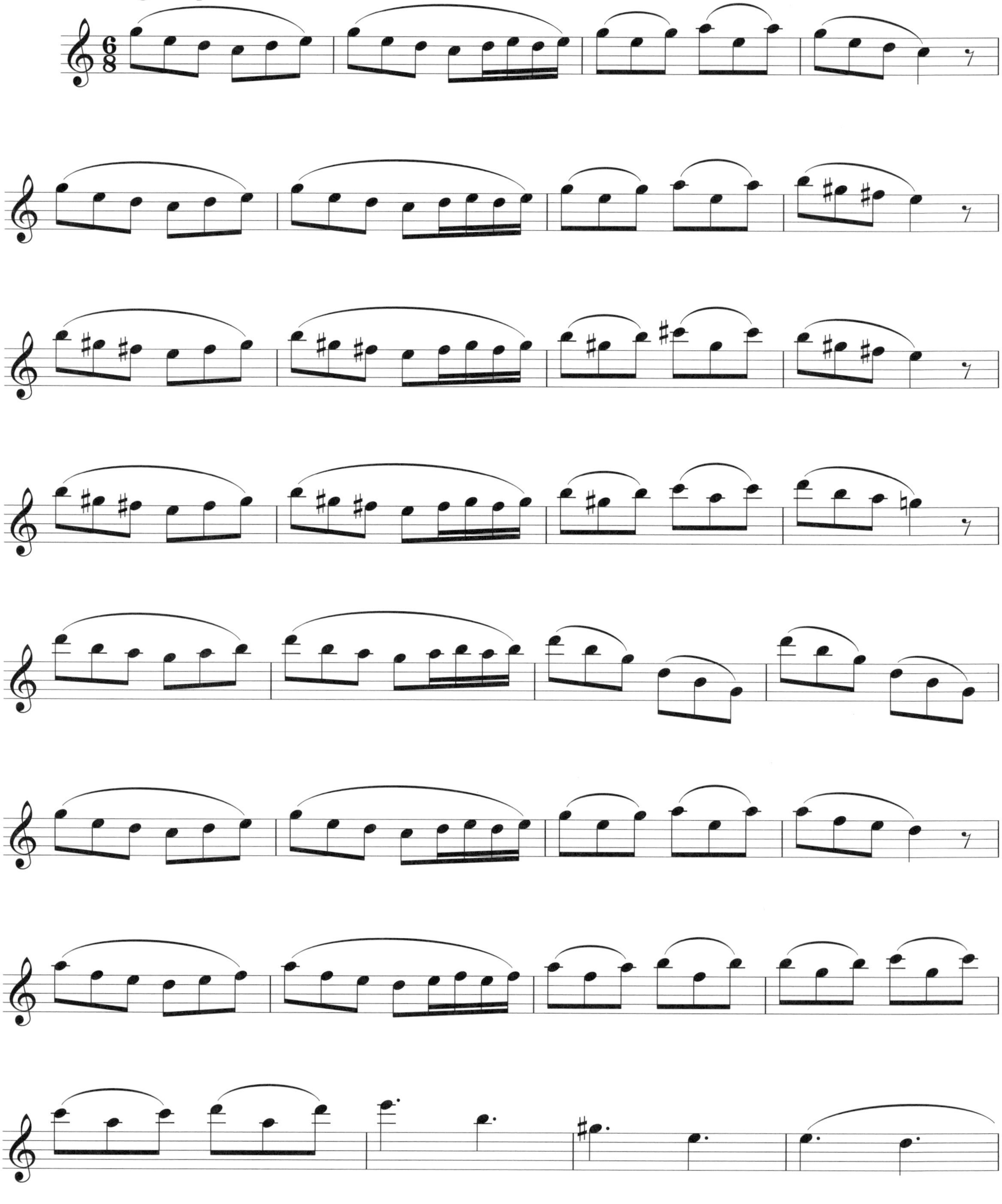

MINUET IN G

from ANNA MAGDALENA NOTEBOOK

JOHANN SEBASTIAN BACH

Moderately

MINUET IN G

FLUTE

LUDWIG VAN BEETHOVEN

ODE TO JOY

from SYMPHONY NO. 9

LUDWIG VAN BEETHOVEN

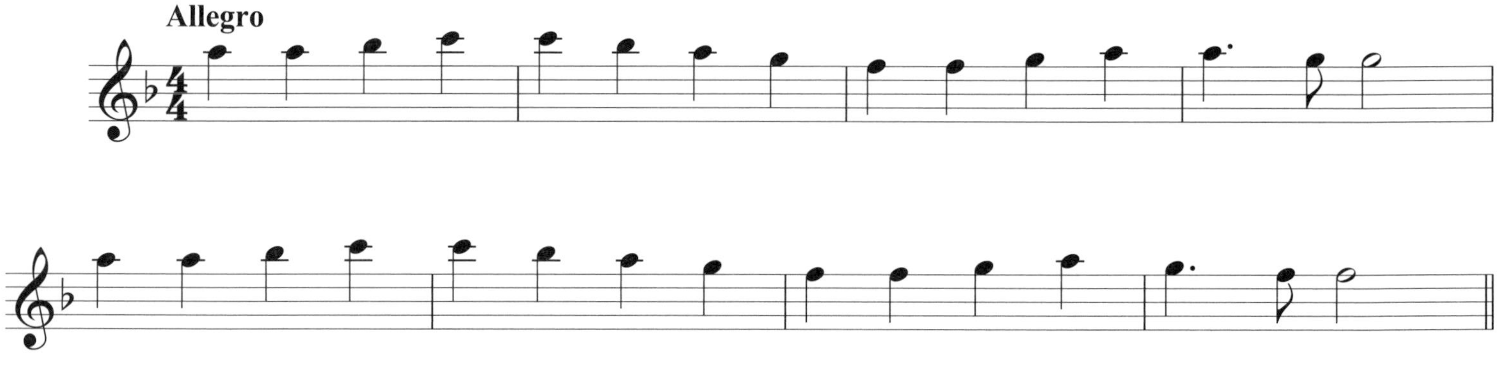

PANIS ANGELICUS

CESAR FRANCK

PIANO SONATA NO. 8: "PATHÉTIQUE"

(Second Movement Theme)

FLUTE

LUDWIG VAN BEETHOVEN

PIANO CONCERTO IN A MINOR

(First Movement Theme)

EDVARD GRIEG

PIANO CONCERTO NO. 21
(Second Movement Theme)

WOLFGANG AMADEUS MOZART

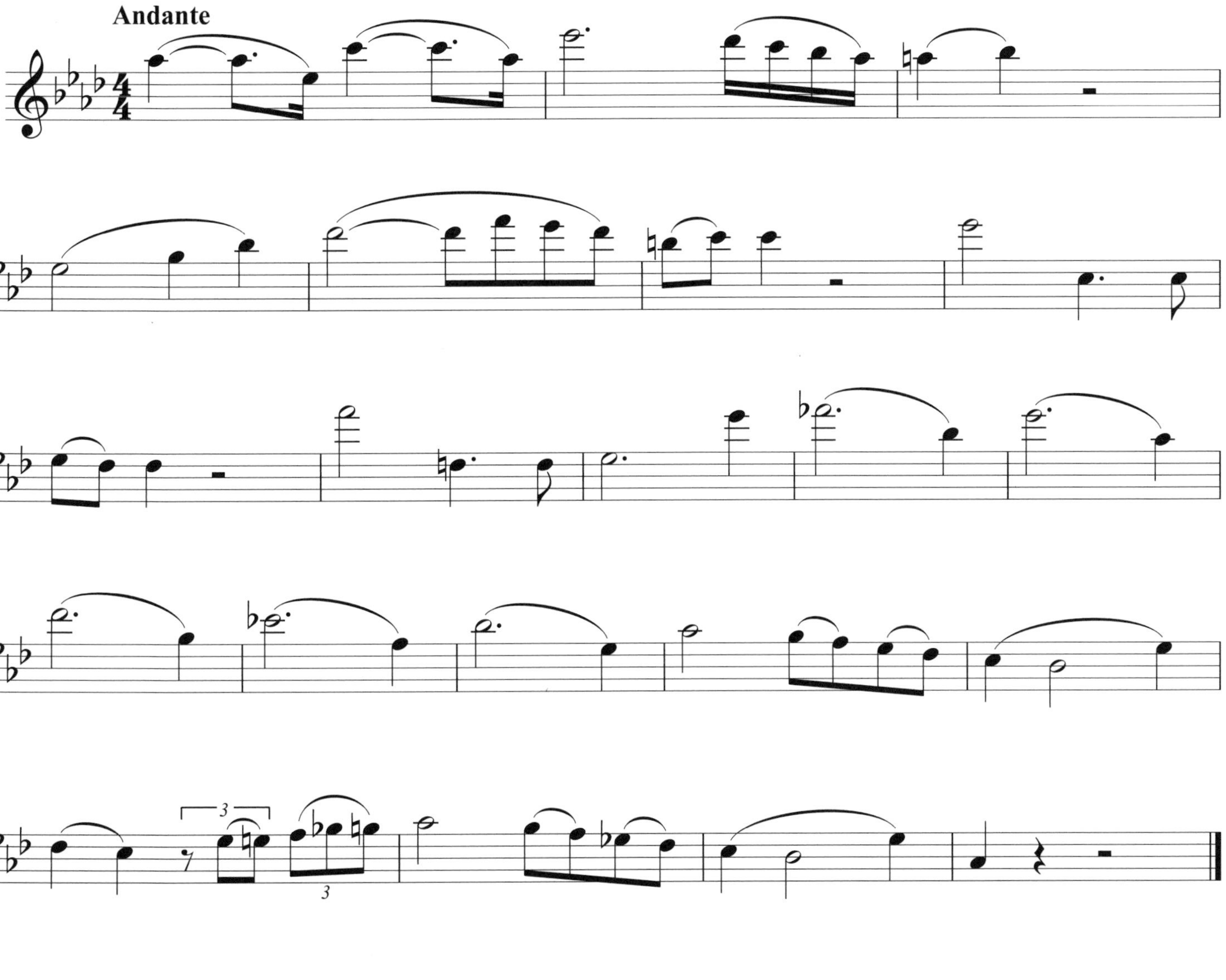

PAVANE

FLUTE

GABRIEL FAURÉ

PIE JESU

from REQUIEM

FLUTE

GABRIEL FAURÉ

PIANO SONATA IN C MAJOR

(First Movement Theme)

FLUTE

WOLFGANG AMADEUS MOZART

PRELUDE IN A MAJOR, OP. 28, NO. 7

FRÉDÉRIC CHOPIN

POLOVETZIAN DANCE

from PRINCE IGOR

FLUTE

ALEXANDER BORODIN

PRELUDE IN C MINOR, OP. 28, NO. 20

FLUTE

FRÉDÉRIC CHOPIN

SINFONIA

from CHRISTMAS ORATORIO

JOHANN SEBASTIAN BACH

ROMEO AND JULIET

(Love Theme)

FLUTE

PYOTR IL'YICH TCHAIKOVSKY

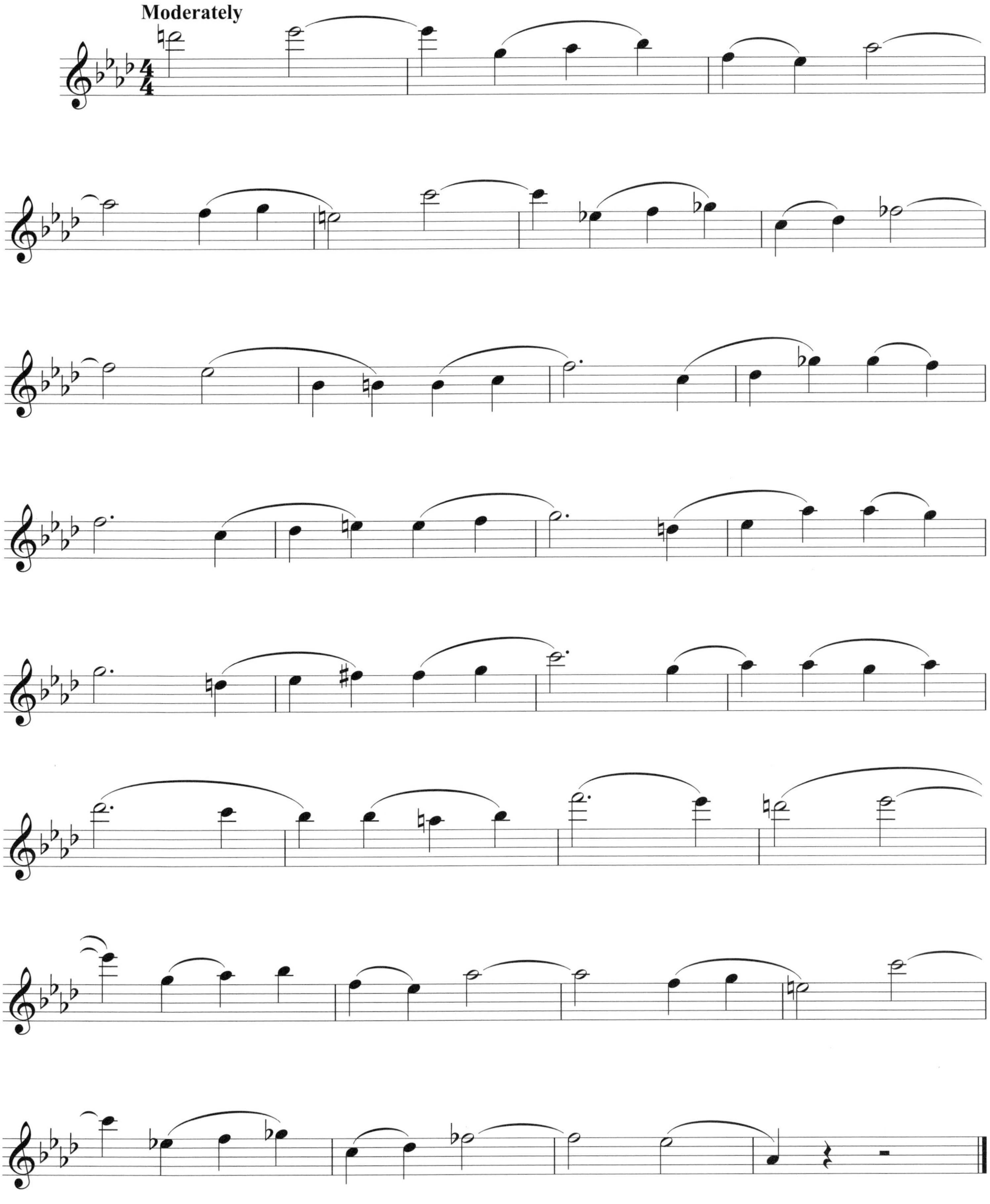

POMP AND CIRCUMSTANCE

FLUTE

EDWARD ELGAR

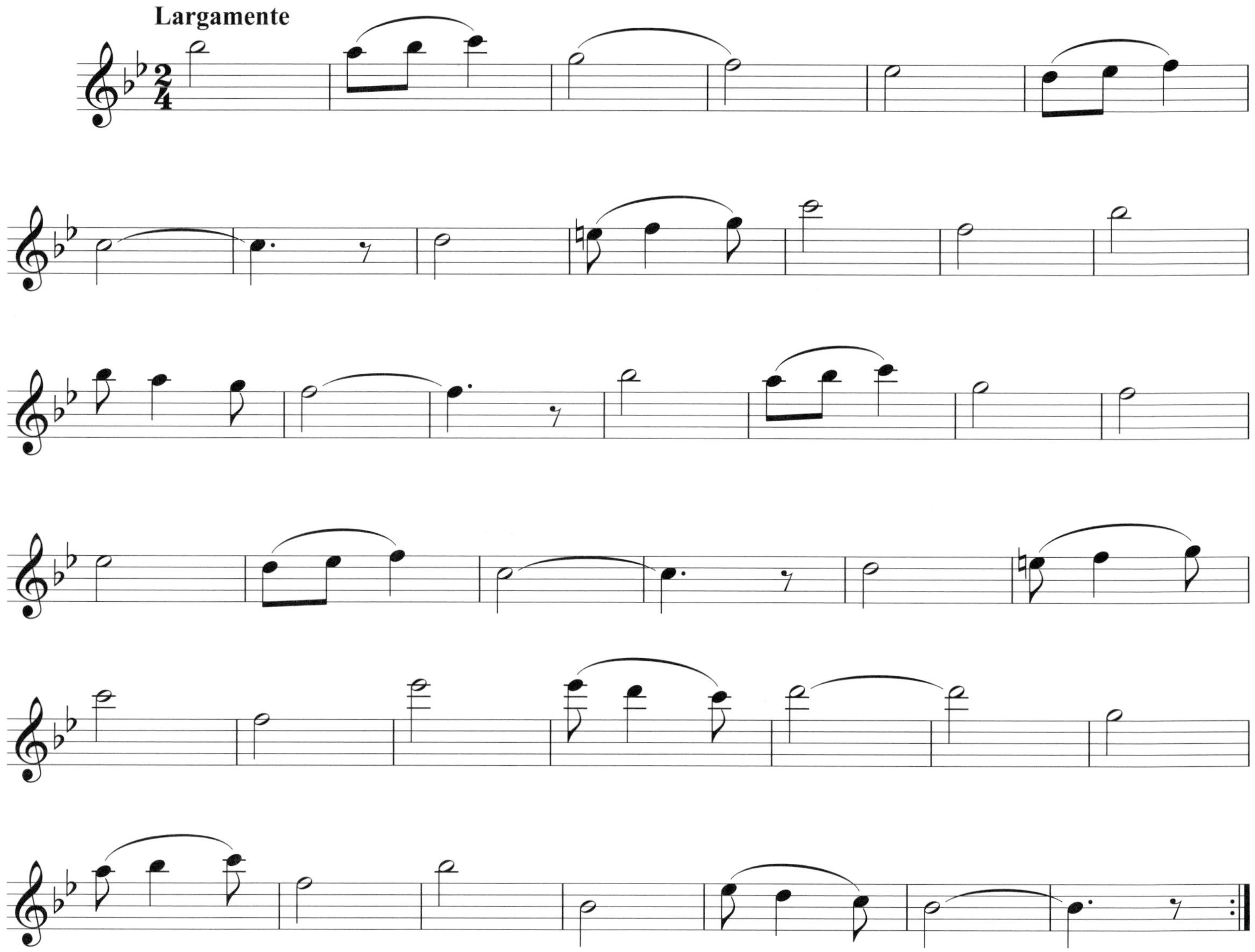

RONDEAU

JEAN-JOSEPH MOURET

RONDO ALLA TURCA

from PIANO SONATA NO. 11

WOLFGANG AMADEUS MOZART

SHEEP MAY SAFELY GRAZE

from CANTATA 208

FLUTE

JOHANN SEBASTIAN BACH

Moderately

THE SORCERER'S APPRENTICE

(Theme)

PAUL DUKAS

March tempo, in 1

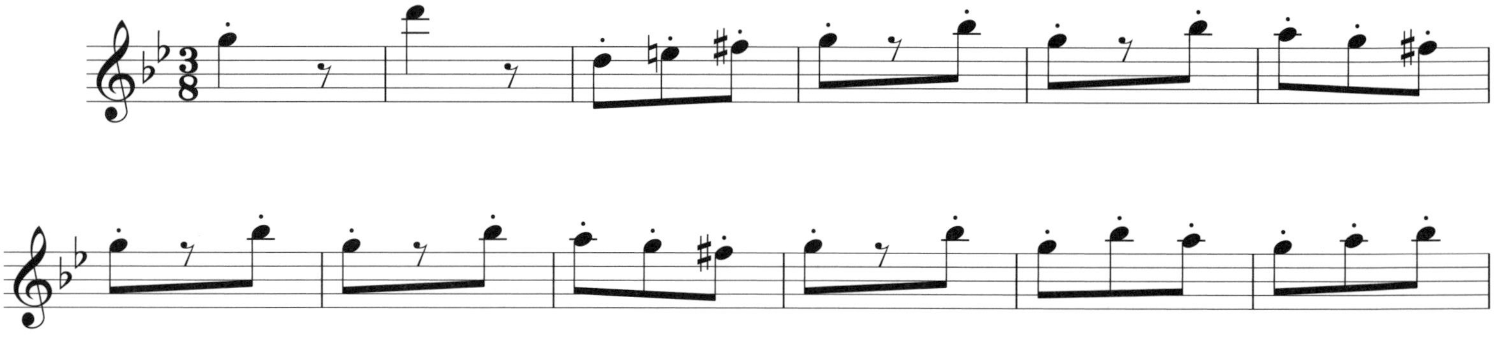

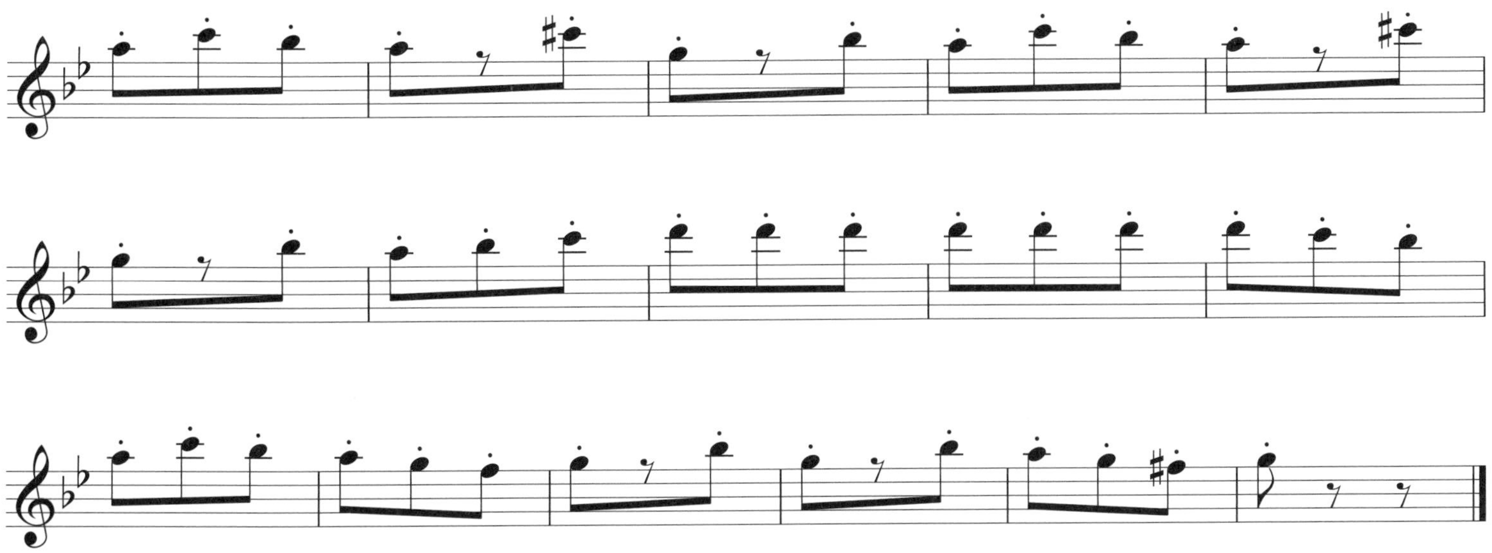

SPRING

from THE FOUR SEASONS
(First Movement Theme)

ANTONIO VIVALDI

SICILIANO

from FLUTE SONATA NO. 2

FLUTE

JOHANN SEBASTIAN BACH

SKATERS WALTZ

FLUTE

ÉMILE WALDTEUFEL

SLEEPERS, AWAKE

from CANTATA 140

FLUTE

JOHANN SEBASTIAN BACH

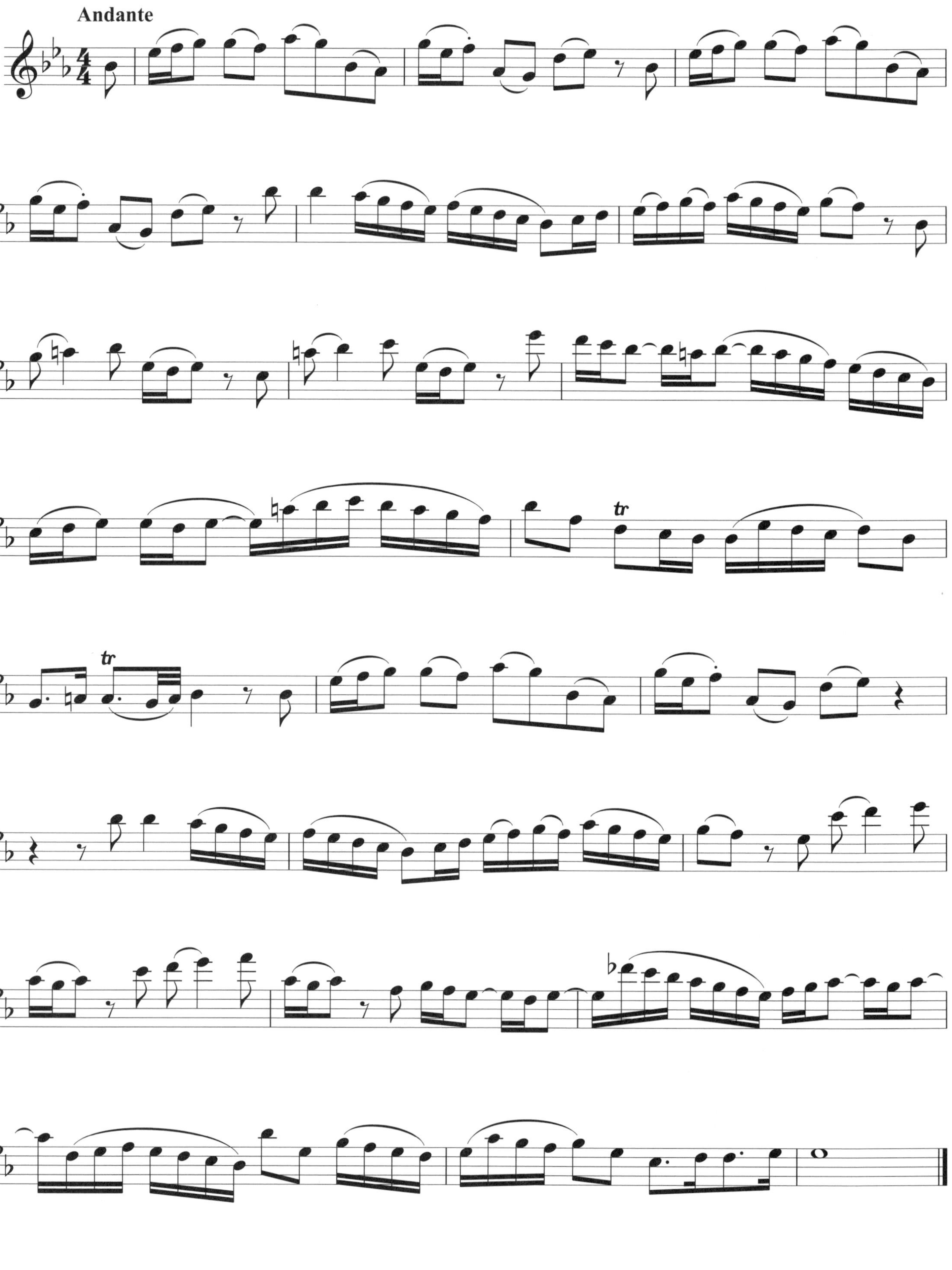

SPINNING SONG

FLUTE

ALBERT ELLMENREICH

SWAN LAKE

(Theme)

FLUTE

PYOTR IL'YICH TCHAIKOVSKY

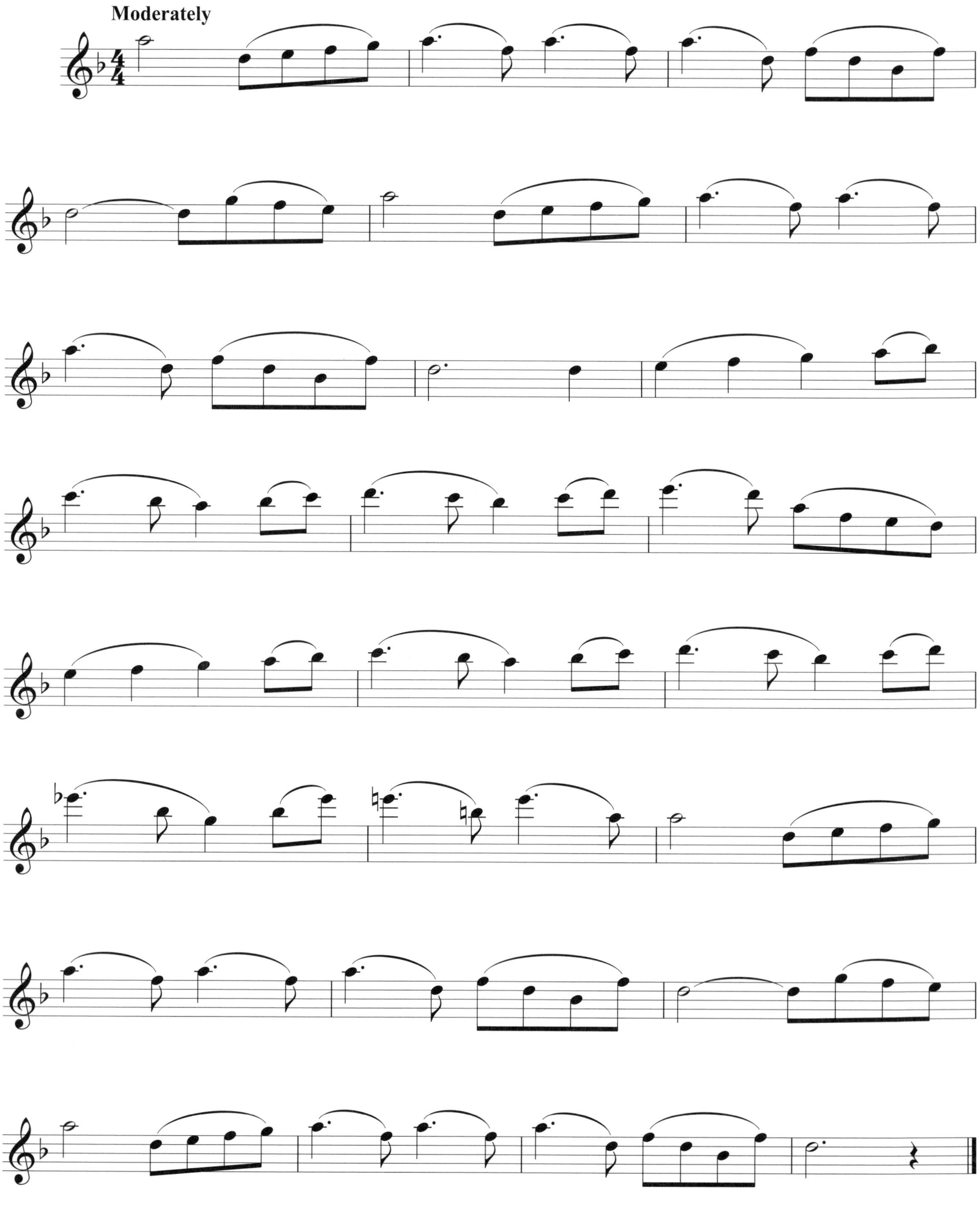

SYMPHONY NO. 5

(First Movement Theme)

FLUTE

LUDWIG VAN BEETHOVEN

Allegro con brio

SYMPHONY NO. 1

(Fourth Movement Theme)

FLUTE

JOHANNES BRAHMS

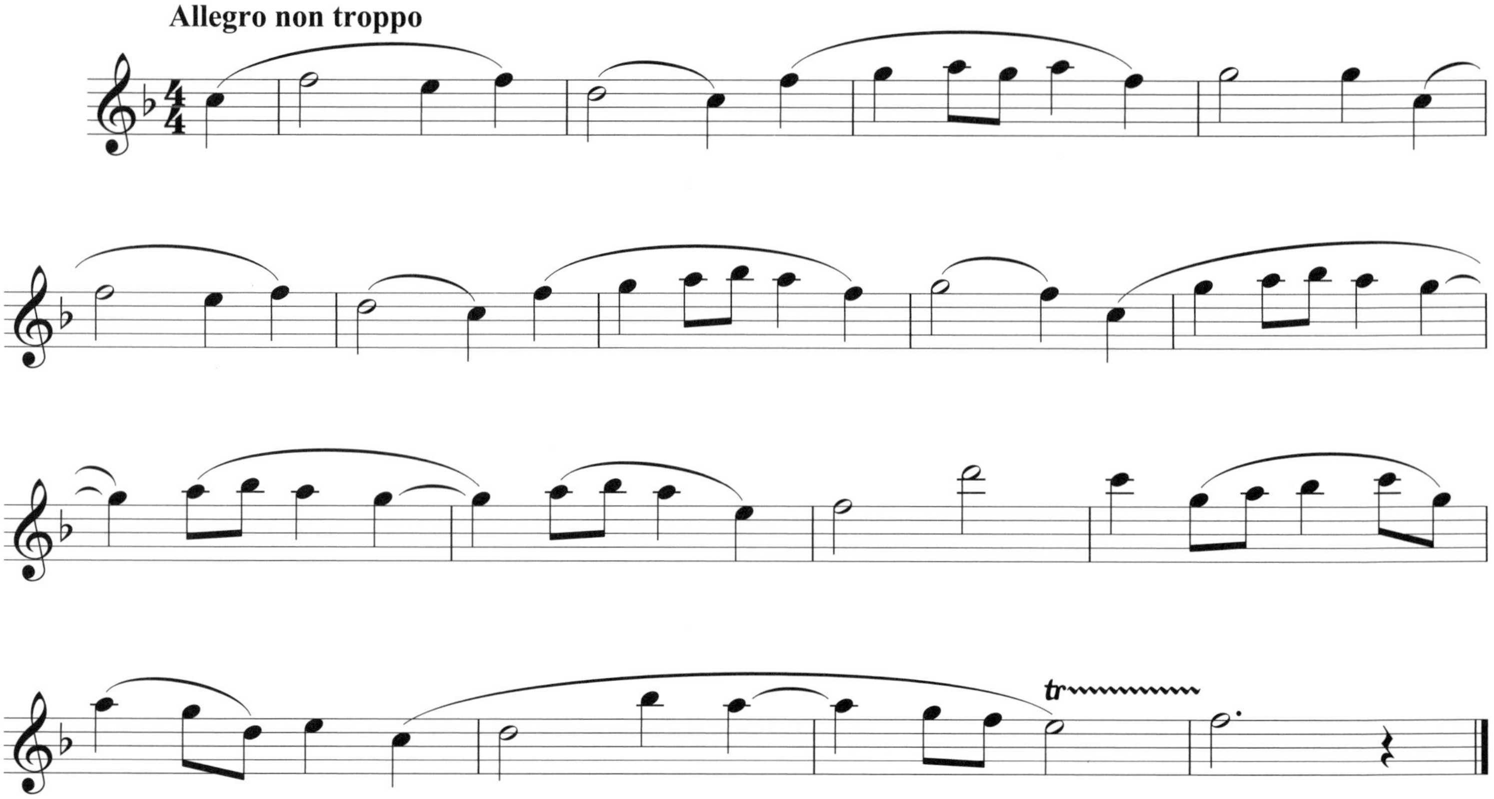
Allegro non troppo
tr

SYMPHONY NO. 7

(Second Movement Theme)

LUDWIG VAN BEETHOVEN

Allegretto

SYMPHONY NO. 9

"From the New World"
(Second Movement Theme)

ANTONÍN DVOŘÁK

SYMPHONY NO. 40

(First Movement Theme)

FLUTE

WOLFGANG AMADEUS MOZART

SYMPHONY NO. 40

(Third Movement Theme)

FLUTE

WOLFGANG AMADEUS MOZART

TALES FROM THE VIENNA WOODS

FLUTE

JOHANN STRAUSS, JR.

TO A WILD ROSE

from WOODLAND SKETCHES

FLUTE

EDWARD MACDOWELL

Moderately, tenderly

SURPRISE SYMPHONY

(Symphony No. 94, Second Movement Theme)

FLUTE

FRANZ JOSEPH HAYDN

TRÄUMERAI

from SCENES FROM CHILDHOOD

ROBERT SCHUMANN

TRUMPET TUNE

HENRY PURCELL

TRUMPET VOLUNTARY

(Prince of Denmark's March)

FLUTE

JEREMIAH CLARKE

WILLIAM TELL OVERTURE

(Theme)

FLUTE

GIOACHINO ROSSINI

FLUTE

UNFINISHED SYMPHONY

(Symphony No. 8)
(First Movement Theme)

FRANZ SCHUBERT

Allegro moderato

WALTZ OF THE FLOWERS

from THE NUTCRACKER

PYOTR IL'YICH TCHAIKOVSKY

Waltz tempo

WALTZ IN C-SHARP MINOR, OP. 64, NO. 2

FLUTE

FRÉDÉRIC CHOPIN

Waltz tempo

TOREADOR SONG

from CARMEN

FLUTE

GEORGES BIZET

WEDDING MARCH

from A MIDSUMMER NIGHT'S DREAM

FELIX MENDELSSOHN

WHERE'ER YOU WALK

from SEMELE

FLUTE

GEORGE FRIDERIC HANDEL

THE WILD HORSEMAN

from ALBUM FOR THE YOUNG

ROBERT SCHUMANN

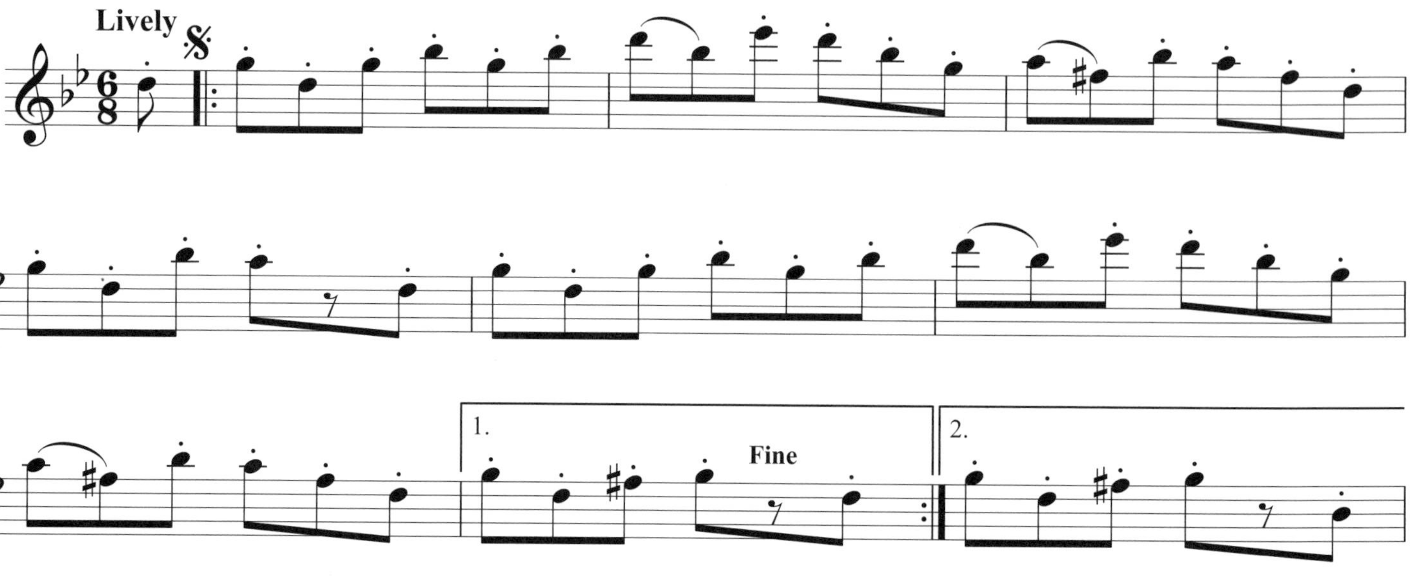

D.S. al Fine
(take 1st ending)

WINTER

from THE FOUR SEASONS
(Second Movement Theme)

ANTONIO VIVALDI

Largo
tr
tr
tr

HAL•LEONARD INSTRUMENTAL PLAY-ALONG

Your favorite songs are arranged just for solo instrumentalists with this outstanding series. Each book includes great full-accompaniment play-along audio so you can sound just like a pro!

Check out **halleonard.com** for songlists, more titles, or to order online from your favorite music retailer.

12 Pop Hits
12 songs • $14.99 each
00261790 Flute · 00261795 Horn
00261791 Clarinet · 00261796 Trombone
00261792 Alto Sax · 00261797 Violin
00261793 Tenor Sax · 00261798 Viola
00261794 Trumpet · 00261799 Cello

The Very Best of Bach
15 selections • $12.99 each
00225371 Flute · 00225376 Horn
00225372 Clarinet · 00225377 Trombone
00225373 Alto Sax · 00225378 Violin
00225374 Tenor Sax · 00225379 Viola
00225375 Trumpet · 00225380 Cello

The Beatles
15 songs • $14.99 each
00225330 Flute · 00225335 Horn
00225331 Clarinet · 00225336 Trombone
00225332 Alto Sax · 00225337 Violin
00225333 Tenor Sax · 00225338 Viola
00225334 Trumpet · 00225339 Cello

Chart Hits
12 songs • $14.99 each
00146207 Flute · 00146212 Horn
00146208 Clarinet · 00146213 Trombone
00146209 Alto Sax · 00146214 Violin
00146210 Tenor Sax · 00146215 Viola
00146211 Trumpet · 00146216 Cello

Christmas Songs
12 songs • $12.99 each
00146855 Flute · 00146863 Horn
00146858 Clarinet · 00146864 Trombone
00146859 Alto Sax · 00146866 Violin
00146860 Tenor Sax · 00146867 Viola
00146862 Trumpet · 00146868 Cello

Contemporary Broadway
15 songs • $14.99 each
00298704 Flute · 00298709 Horn
00298705 Clarinet · 00298710 Trombone
00298706 Alto Sax · 00298711 Violin
00298707 Tenor Sax · 00298712 Viola
00298708 Trumpet · 00298713 Cello

Disney Movie Hits
12 songs • $14.99 each
00841420 Flute · 00841424 Horn
00841687 Oboe · 00841425 Trombone
00841421 Clarinet · 00841426 Violin
00841422 Alto Sax · 00841427 Viola
00841686 Tenor Sax · 00841428 Cello
00841423 Trumpet

Prices, contents, and availability subject to change without notice.

Disney characters and artwork ™ & © 2021 Disney

Disney Solos
12 songs • $14.99 each
00841404 Flute · 00841506 Oboe
00841406 Alto Sax · 0841409 Trumpet
00841407 Horn · 00841410 Violin
00841411 Viola · 00841412 Cello
00841405 Clarinet/Tenor Sax
00841408 Trombone/Baritone
00841553 Mallet Percussion

Dixieland Favorites
15 songs • $12.99 each
00268756 Flute · 0068759 Trumpet
00268757 Clarinet · 00268760 Trombone
00268758 Alto Sax

Billie Eilish
9 songs • $14.99 each
00345648 Flute · 00345653 Horn
00345649 Clarinet · 00345654 Trombone
00345650 Alto Sax · 00345655 Violin
00345651 Tenor Sax · 00345656 Viola
00345652 Trumpet · 00345657 Cello

Favorite Movie Themes
13 songs • $14.99 each
00841166 Flute · 00841168 Trumpet
00841167 Clarinet · 00841170 Trombone
00841169 Alto Sax · 00841296 Violin

Gospel Hymns
15 songs • $12.99 each
00194648 Flute · 00194654 Trombone
00194649 Clarinet · 00194655 Violin
00194650 Alto Sax · 00194656 Viola
00194651 Tenor Sax · 00194657 Cello
00194652 Trumpet

Great Classical Themes
15 songs • $12.99 each
00292727 Flute · 00292733 Horn
00292728 Clarinet · 00292735 Trombone
00292729 Alto Sax · 00292736 Violin
00292730 Tenor Sax · 00292737 Viola
00292732 Trumpet · 00292738 Cello

The Greatest Showman
8 songs • $14.99 each
00277389 Flute · 00277394 Horn
00277390 Clarinet · 00277395 Trombone
00277391 Alto Sax · 00277396 Violin
00277392 Tenor Sax · 00277397 Viola
00277393 Trumpet · 00277398 Cello

Irish Favorites
31 songs • $12.99 each
00842489 Flute · 00842495 Trombone
00842490 Clarinet · 00842496 Violin
00842491 Alto Sax · 00842497 Viola
00842493 Trumpet · 00842498 Cello
00842494 Horn

Michael Jackson
11 songs • $14.99 each
00119495 Flute · 00119499 Trumpet
00119496 Clarinet · 00119501 Trombone
00119497 Alto Sax · 00119503 Violin
00119498 Tenor Sax · 00119502 Accomp.

Jazz & Blues
14 songs • $14.99 each
00841438 Flute · 00841441 Trumpet
00841439 Clarinet · 00841443 Trombone
00841440 Alto Sax · 00841444 Violin
00841442 Tenor Sax

Jazz Classics
12 songs • $12.99 each
00151812 Flute · 00151816 Trumpet
00151813 Clarinet · 00151818 Trombone
00151814 Alto Sax · 00151819 Violin
00151815 Tenor Sax · 00151821 Cello

Les Misérables
13 songs • $14.99 each
00842292 Flute · 00842297 Horn
00842293 Clarinet · 00842298 Trombone
00842294 Alto Sax · 00842299 Violin
00842295 Tenor Sax · 00842300 Viola
00842296 Trumpet · 00842301 Cello

Metallica
12 songs • $14.99 each
02501327 Flute · 02502454 Horn
02501339 Clarinet · 02501329 Trombone
02501332 Alto Sax · 02501334 Violin
02501333 Tenor Sax · 02501335 Viola
02501330 Trumpet · 02501338 Cello

Motown Classics
15 songs • $12.99 each
00842572 Flute · 00842576 Trumpet
00842573 Clarinet · 00842578 Trombone
00842574 Alto Sax · 00842579 Violin
00842575 Tenor Sax

Pirates of the Caribbean
16 songs • $14.99 each
00842183 Flute · 00842188 Horn
00842184 Clarinet · 00842189 Trombone
00842185 Alto Sax · 00842190 Violin
00842186 Tenor Sax · 00842191 Viola
00842187 Trumpet · 00842192 Cello

Queen
17 songs • $14.99 each
00285402 Flute · 00285407 Horn
00285403 Clarinet · 00285408 Trombone
00285404 Alto Sax · 00285409 Violin
00285405 Tenor Sax · 00285410 Viola
00285406 Trumpet · 00285411 Cello

Simple Songs
14 songs • $12.99 each
00249081 Flute · 00249087 Horn
00249092 Oboe · 00249089 Trombone
00249082 Clarinet · 00249090 Violin
00249083 Alto Sax · 00249091 Viola
00249084 Tenor Sax · 00249092 Cello
00249086 Trumpet · 00249094 Mallets

Superhero Themes
14 songs • $14.99 each
00363195 Flute · 00363200 Horn
00363196 Clarinet · 00363201 Trombone
00363197 Alto Sax · 00363202 Violin
00363198 Tenor Sax · 00363203 Viola
00363199 Trumpet · 00363204 Cello

Star Wars
16 songs • $16.99 each
00350900 Flute · 00350907 Horn
00350913 Oboe · 00350908 Trombone
00350903 Clarinet · 00330909 Violin
00350904 Alto Sax · 00350910 Viola
00350905 Tenor Sax · 00350911 Cello
00350906 Trumpet · 00350914 Mallet

Taylor Swift
15 songs • $12.99 each
00842532 Flute · 00842537 Horn
00842533 Clarinet · 00842538 Trombone
00842534 Alto Sax · 00842539 Violin
00842535 Tenor Sax · 00842540 Viola
00842536 Trumpet · 00842541 Cello

Video Game Music
13 songs • $12.99 each
00283877 Flute · 00283883 Horn
00283878 Clarinet · 00283884 Trombone
00283879 Alto Sax · 00283885 Violin
00283880 Tenor Sax · 00283886 Viola
00283882 Trumpet · 00283887 Cello

Wicked
13 songs • $12.99 each
00842236 Flute · 00842241 Horn
00842237 Clarinet · 00842242 Trombone
00842238 Alto Sax · 00842243 Violin
00842239 Tenor Sax · 00842244 Viola
00842240 Trumpet · 00842245 Cello

HAL•LEONARD®

0521
488

HAL•LEONARD

Classical PLAY-ALONG™

The Hal Leonard Classical Play-Along™ series will help you play great classical pieces. Listen to the full performance tracks to hear how the piece sounds with an orchestra, and then play along using the accompaniment tracks. The audio CD is playable on any CD player. For PC and Mac computer users, the CD is enhanced so you can adjust the recording to any tempo without changing pitch.

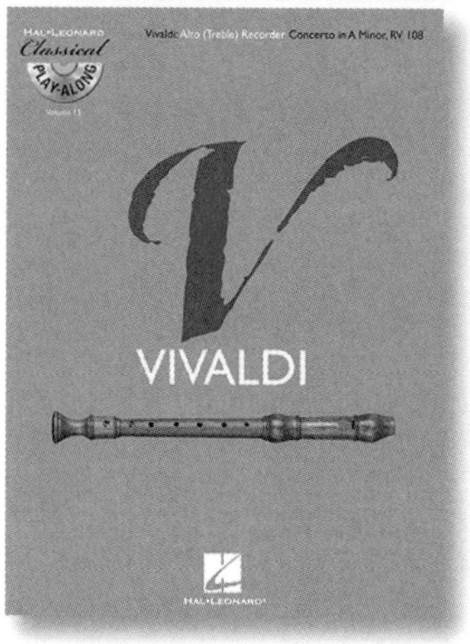

1. MOZART:
FLUTE CONCERTO IN D MAJOR, K314
Book/CD Pack
00842341 Flute....................$12.99

2. SAMMARTINI:
DESCANT (SOPRANO) RECORDER CONCERTO IN F MAJOR
Book/CD Pack
00842342 Soprano Recorder....................$12.99

3. LOEILLET:
TREBLE (ALTO) RECORDER SONATA IN G MAJOR, OP.1, NO.3
Book/CD Pack
00842343 Alto Recorder....................$12.99

4. MOZART:
CLARINET CONCERTO IN A MAJOR, K622
Book/CD Pack
00842344 Clarinet....................$12.99

6. MOZART:
HORN CONCERTO IN D MAJOR, K412/514
Book/CD Pack
00842346 Horn....................$12.99

7. BACH:
VIOLIN CONCERTO IN A MINOR, BWV 1041
Book/CD Pack
00842347 Violin....................$12.99

8. TELEMANN:
VIOLA CONCERTO IN G MAJOR, TWV 51:G9
Book/Online Audio
00842348 Viola....................$12.99

9. HAYDN:
CELLO CONCERTO IN C MAJOR, HOB. VIIB: 1
Book/CD Pack
00842349 Cello....................$12.99

10. BACH:
PIANO CONCERTO IN F MINOR, BWV 1056
Book/CD Pack
00842350 Piano....................$12.99

11. PERGOLESI:
FLUTE CONCERTO IN G MAJOR
Book/CD Pack
00842351 Flute....................$12.99

12. BARRE:
DESCANT (SOPRANO) RECORDER SUITE NO. 9 "DEUXIEME LIVRE" G MAJOR
Book/Online Audio
00842352 Soprano Recorder....................$12.99

14. VON WEBER:
CLARINET CONCERTO NO. 1 IN F MINOR, OP. 73
Book/CD Pack
00842354 Clarinet....................$12.99

15. MOZART:
VIOLIN CONCERTO IN G MAJOR, K216
Book/CD Pack
00842355 Violin....................$12.99

16. BOCCHERINI:
CELLO CONCERTO IN B-FLAT MAJOR, G482
Book/CD Pack
00842356 Cello....................$12.99

17. MOZART:
PIANO CONCERTO IN C MAJOR, K467
Book/CD Pack
00842357 Piano....................$12.99

18. BACH:
FLUTE SONATA IN E-FLAT MAJOR, BWV 1031
Book/CD Pack
00842450 Flute....................$12.99

19. BRAHMS:
CLARINET SONATA IN F MINOR, OP. 120, NO. 1
Book/CD Pack
00842451 Clarinet....................$12.99

20. BEETHOVEN:
TWO ROMANCES FOR VIOLIN, OP. 40 IN G & OP. 50 IN F
Book/CD Pack
00842452 Violin....................$12.99

21. MOZART:
PIANO CONCERTO IN D MINOR, K466
Book/CD Pack
00842453 Piano....................$12.99

Prices, content, and availability subject to change without notice.

HAL•LEONARD®

www.halleonard.com

0419
458